Breaking the

Chains

of

Abuse

How I Survived Domestic Violence

DEDICATION

To my parents, sisters, brother, and aunt who stood by my side throughout this trying time, thank you for always being there. You all have been a shoulder to cry on, a lending ear, and helped to keep me grounded when I didn't know what to do.

To my beautiful daughters, the both of you gave me the strength, determination, and the courage to leave. Without the two of you, there is no me.

Breaking The Chains of Abuse

How I Survived Domestic Violence

Prologue

The COVID-19 pandemic heightened incidents of domestic violence worldwide. During the quarantine, because there was no option but to stay inside – the abuser had more chances to control the victim. While domestic violence remains significantly underreported, the number of incidents reported to the police showed an increase during the pandemic.

Domestic violence is a tragic reality for many victims around the world. In general, domestic violence is abuse that occurs in a domestic setting such as in marriage, cohabitation, or between intimate partners. Domestic violence is committed by one person against another with victims including, but certainly not limited to: children, spouses, the elderly, and parents.

The forms and degree of domestic violence can vary greatly. Physical, verbal, sexual, emotional, and financial violence are among the most common types. Overwhelmingly, the victims of domestic violence in the world are women. The effects of domestic violence can be severe and long-lasting.

Domestic violence and/or abuse affects men, women, or teen girls and boys, whether in a married or unmarried, straight, or same-sex relationship. Domestic violence may consist of one or more forms, including emotional, psychological, physical, sexual, or economic abuse, and is defined as one person in an intimate relationship using any means to put down or otherwise control the other. Types of domestic abuse include physical, verbal, sexual, economic/financial, and spiritual abuse.

- In the United States, an average of 20 people per minute are physically abused by close partners. In a year, this represents more than 10 million women and men.
- 1 in 4 women and 1 in 9 men have exposure to severe physical violence from intimate partners, sexual violence from intimate partners, and/or intimate partner stalking. Some impacts include injuries, fears, post-traumatic stress disorder, use of victim services, the onset of sexually transmitted diseases, etc.

- 1 in 15 children are exposed to intimate partner violence each year, and 90% of these children are eyewitnesses to this violence
- In domestic violence homicides, women are six times more likely to be killed when there is a gun in the house
- Intimate partner violence accounts for 15% of all violent crime

Domestic violence is a learned behavior by the abuser. After witnessing patterns of domestic violence from their families, friends, or societal influences, people may develop and repeat the same patterns over time. Remember that domestic violence is never the victim's fault, no matter what.

Introduction

My name is L. Anderson, I am a forty-one-year-old mother of two beautiful girls. I work a full-time job for an automotive retailer, and I am learning to live a normal, stress-free life, although it hasn't always been that way, however, I am making the best of it. I would like to share a little about the struggle I dealt with for 13 years. I've always wanted to tell my story, but it wasn't until now that I regained my voice and gained the courage to do so.

I never thought that I would become part of a statistic where I suffered from physical, mental, verbal, and sexual abuse. As I look back on the things that were meant to tear me down, I realize that God was always there to bring me out. I was put in the position to go thru my situation so that I can help others get out, as well as help those on the outside looking in identify the ways to better help someone going through domestic violence.

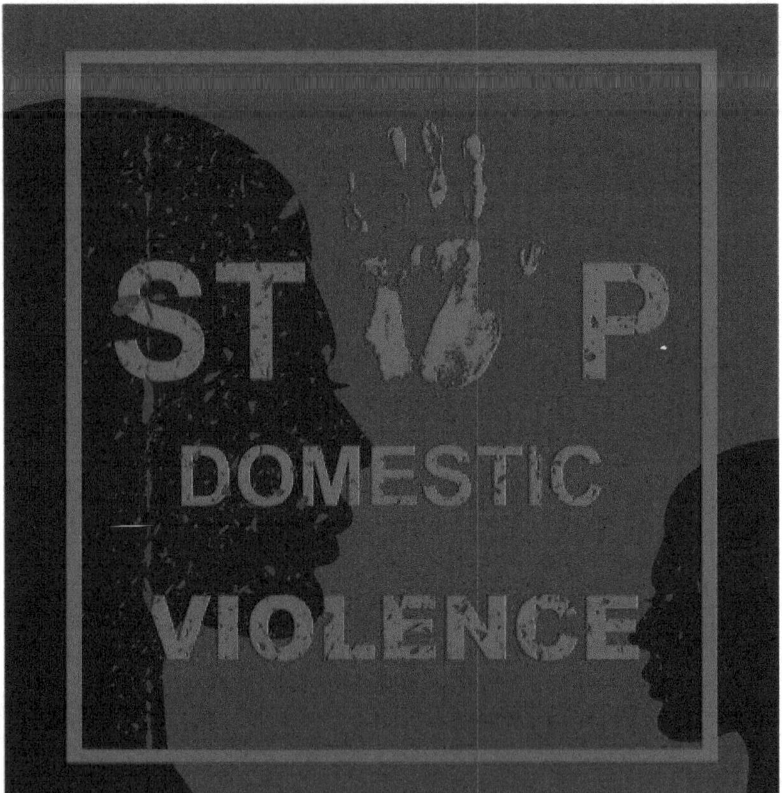
ST P
DOMESTIC
VIOLENCE

Table of Contents

After 13 years of being abused, I finally had the courage to leave. Taking back my power, my joy, my life, and finding peace that surpasses all understanding.

Listening to the Word of God

~ If God keeps taking me out of a toxic situation, but I keep running back to it there was no way he can bring me out of it. ~

Sometimes you think God is not going to come thru for you, he doesn't see what you had to go thru; or that God has forgotten all about you. God said no I have had my hands and eyes on you. You just had to get on my time, get into a position for what I was getting ready to do. You thought I left you because of what you were going through, I will never leave you and this is my promise to you.

There were so many times I questioned myself, wondering how in the hell did I allow myself to be in an abusive relationship? I didn't grow up seeing or experiencing abuse from my parents or family members. Just knowing I was going thru domestic violence had me in complete disbelief. Often, I would ask God, "Why am I in this predicament" or ask God to give me a way out. God told me these are the times I gave you a way out:

1. When he choked you and held you over a rail, you left with your child and the clothes on your back. You went back to him.
2. He stomped you while you were holding your child and held your head under water. You had an opportunity to leave, but you went back.
3. He sliced your hands and face with a knife. You went to the police station but didn't follow thru and you went back.
4. He held a gun to your face, and the police came and instructed him to leave. You let him back in.
5. He pushed you into a counter causing bleeding around the brain and faced jail time. You went back to him

God said he will never leave me nor forsake me, and I needed to trust Him. At this point, I knew if God kept taking me out of a toxic situation, but I kept running back to it, there was no way he could bring me out of it. This meant there was no turning back, if I wanted a life where my children and I were free from abuse I had to stand firm and not give in to the threats or intimidation from Maurice.

God says you have to go thru the storm to understand the power you have to get thru it. You had to go thru it and feel like you weren't going to make it. This is your test, this is your trial, and you will come out not looking like what you went through.

I am so glad that I don't look like what I have been thru. I kept my faith and trust in God, he made sure that he did not leave me like I was, and he did not forsake me. I may have lost my home and my marriage, but I never lost my faith and trust in God. He allowed me to overcome domestic violence and didn't allow it to destroy me. What the devil meant for bad, God meant for my good. I'm here to tell you that no matter what you are going thru God will see you through. See this test was my storm and God had something better for me in store. The chains of abuse have been broken and I am now free. My testimony is how I survived domestic violence, now my mission is to encourage others to get out of their abusive situation. As you read my story you will see how I overcame the obstacles, broke the chain of abuse, and how survived domestic violence.

The Meet-Up

November 2005, as I was driving down American Way, I made a stop at the red light. In the car next to me were two men flagging me down. I let the passenger side window down as the driver began conversing with me. The light began to turn green, and the driver indicated he wanted me to pull over to the parking lot of the grocery store to finish conversing. I pulled over to the parking lot and Maurice climbed in the passenger side of my car. I realized he was intoxicated as he tried to tell me about the night he just had and tell me about himself. We exchanged phone numbers and agreed to meet up again later. A month later we met up and began dating. Everything was going great, and Maurice was the perfect gentleman. As several months passed Maurice invited me to live with him; I excitedly obliged. Things were going well as we became one household until a few months had passed. As time went on things began to change; Maurice would stay out late indicating he was out with his cousins, so I would go to bed and wake up through the night until he made it home.

This night, Maurice came home around 2 am intoxicated and began talking crazy. He began to yell, curse, and become belligerent. I got up to go to the bathroom and he grabbed me by the throat holding me over the balcony. I pulled his hands from around my neck and went into the bathroom. Around 10 minutes later Maurice was lying in bed sleeping. I grabbed some of my things and left his house. When Maurice awoke the next morning, he called me, but I didn't answer. This went on for 2 days until I finally answered. Maurice asked why I left, and I told him what he had done. He became very apologetic saying he didn't remember doing anything that night. He assured me that it would never happen again, so I agreed to come back. For the next couple of months, everything was perfect, and Maurice stuck to his word and became the perfect man until he kept meeting up with his cousins Bernard and Corey.

At the end of April 2006, as Maurice and I were having dinner there was a knock on the door. Maurice opened the door and Corey came running in saying a girl, one of Bernard's friends, braided his hair and he ran off not paying her. Around midnight the girl came back knocking on the neighbor's door, thinking she was at the right house, robbing him. The next night, Maurice left for work around 7 pm, telling me to ensure the house was locked up and he would talk to me on the phone all night to make sure I was safe. While over the road Maurice called stating he was at the weigh station and his license had been suspended. His freight company had to get someone to pick him up and bring him back home. Once Maurice arrived home, he began to hang out with his cousins again. This night was a little different than others. While at Bernard's house, Bernard asked Maurice to pick up a friend from a motel. As Maurice went into the motel to pick up the girl he was shot.

The Setup

On May 2nd I was awakened by a phone call. Maurice stated he had been shot and was in the hospital. I jumped out of bed, gathered my belongings, and rushed to the hospital. Maurice underwent surgery and was placed in ICU. After three days he was allowed to have visitors, so I came to visit and brought one of his friends to see him as well. Maurice put everyone out of the room, grabbed me, and accused me of being with his friend. I snatched it away from him, and the doctor came in to check on him. The doctor informed Maurice that he was doing fine, he had a long road to recovery, but he had a significant amount of cocaine in his system. Maurice insisted he didn't do any drugs and that he only touched it and that was the reason it was in his system. The next day I visited Maurice, while there a young lady came into his room with a care package stating she had been there the day before to clean him up. I left the hospital saying I was done with him. A little over two months passed and I began receiving calls from Maurice. He apologized, said he missed me, and insisted he needed my help. I went to visit him at the hospital, where I stayed the night with him. He had a complete change of heart. We began to read the Bible and pray with each other every night. I gave him my address and he came over needing me to change his bandages. Maurice stayed the night and ended up living with me.

A few months later I was scheduled to have surgery. Maurice left the night before and never showed up for the surgery. He left town with his brother to return a few days later. I packed all his belongings into trash bags, placed them by the front door, and left the house. When I returned home, I realized Maurice had been there, he cut up my clothes, set them on fire, and placed them in the shower. I reached out to him to see why he did those things, again he apologized saying, "I didn't mean to, I thought you were leaving me, and I will never do it again." Being so naïve, I forgave him.

In April 2007, I began working for an automotive company as a manager. Within a month of working, I learned I was pregnant. I informed Maurice of the news and he was ecstatic. The next day, I got up to go to work, realizing Maurice was gone in my car I decided to drive his. I informed him that he did not have gas in the car, and he told me to come straight to the house, so I did as he requested. When I made it to the house Maurice decided to leave again, but this time in his car. Before leaving I reminded him that he needed gas leaving. Either he didn't listen, didn't remember, or didn't care because Maurice left and never put gas in the car. He ended up pushing the car to the gas station, getting gas, and going out with his friends. When Maurice made it home, he was highly intoxicated and now extremely mad due to him running out of gas. He became irate, slapped me, and punched me in the stomach. I rolled up into a ball and began to cry letting him know that he may have harmed the baby, but he didn't care. He continued to yell at me while saying it was my fault, he hit me. I lay in bed crying, praying, and asking God why I was in this situation. The next morning Maurice woke up and I told him everything he did, but of course, I got the same thing, he didn't remember doing any of it and he was apologetic; yet I continued to accept his apology. As time went on Maurice calmed down and the physical abuse dwindled, that was until after the birth of our daughter.

Under the Influence

~I fell to the floor, and he began stomping me in the head and stomach while I was holding my 2-year-old in my arms, protecting her from inadvertently being kicked. ~

January 2008, I gave birth to our daughter. Everything was going great until Maurice realized that we could not have intercourse for six weeks after the birth of our child. Although I knew I shouldn't have, he insisted that we have sex. He continued to become irate until I finally had to give in to what he wanted. As weeks turned into months, we decided to let people see our girls. It started with only his family being able to see the girls until I convinced Maurice to let my baby go to my sister's house. While the baby was at my sister's house she was inadvertently burned with an iron. Maurice picked her up from my sister's house and upon seeing the burn, he instantly took it out on me. While I was lying in bed he reached over and punched me in the face. He dragged me out of the bed by my hair, I fell to the floor, and he began stomping me in the head and stomach while I was holding my 2-year-old in my arms, protecting her from inadvertently being kicked. After about a minute, which felt like a lifetime, he grabbed me by the hair, drug me into the bathroom, and forced my head under the faucet in the bathtub. He began running water over my face attempting to drown me. Maurice finally stopped and decided to go to sleep. The next morning, I went to his mother's house, and she took me to the emergency room. The police were called, a statement was made, and however, nothing was done to Maurice.

Several months later I decided to go back to college. On the day of my orientation, Maurice came home from being out all night, high and intoxicated. He looked at the shirt that I had on and said, "Bitch take that off." As I proceeded to change clothes Maurice came in with a knife saying, "call the cops because I'm going to kill you." He came towards me with the knife and as he charged towards me aiming for my neck, I put up my hand and wound up being cut across my face and hand. He then grabbed me by the throat, laid down on the bed, and went to sleep. I looked at him while he was sleeping and noticed a white substance coming from his nose, this is when I realized he had been snorting cocaine. I eased away from under him, grabbed my keys, and went to the police station. I made a report and pictures were taken of my injuries: however, the police never contacted me to follow up on the incident.

A few days later, I went to work, and we were short-staffed. The store manager asked me to pick up one of our coworkers to assist with the current shift. I went to pick up my coworker, just so happened, that Maurice called the store while I was out. When I made it home from work Maurice asked me where I had been, and I told him I had to pick up a coworker for them to work a shift. He asked the person's name and I let him know who it was, a male, he became pissed and punched me in the face. He then took my phone and broke it, grabbed his gun put it on my head saying he would kill me if I did it again. He then grabbed my broken phone, my keys to my house and car, and left the house. Being in fear for my life I emailed my daycare provider and a few friends requesting them to contact the police. When Maurice arrived back at the house the police came and told him he needed to leave the house for the night. I began to think calling the police was a waste of time since nothing was ever done to him.

Bleeding Around the Brain

~I was rushed to the hospital where they found bleeding around my brain~

Maurice decided he wanted to go out with his friends. I was fine with it because it allowed me to have free time with the kids in peace. After cooking, cleaning, and getting the girls ready for bed; I fell asleep around 9 pm since I had to be at work early the next morning. Maurice called around 9:15 saying he was on his way home; however, he didn't show up until6 am the next morning. When he made it home, he was drunk and high off cocaine. Maurice woke me from my sleep asking for my bank card. He said if you don't have any money in your account, you're dead, he was belligerent, and constantly making threats. I got up, headed towards the front of the house, grabbed my purse, and handed him my bank card. While he wasn't paying attention, I ran into the kitchen and pressed the panic code on the alarm system. He walked to the alarm system and began yelling, "hoe why the fuck are you pressing the alarm," all while tussling attempting to turn it off using the normal passcode to keep from notifying the police. Maurice shoved me causing me to hit my head on the counter, pushing the counter over some and passing out. While I was knocked out, he turned off the alarm, took my bank card, and ran away from the house to keep from being caught by the police. When I came to, his daughter, my two children, his mother, the police, my aunt, and the paramedics were standing around.

I was rushed to the hospital where they found bleeding around my brain. I was in the hospital for a couple of days before being released to go home with my aunt. She made sure that I had everything I needed and that my children were ok. I felt like I was at my lowest point, and I couldn't do anything for myself. This injury took a lot out of me, it hurt to talk and even to think. So, I decided to call my mom and have her come to my aunt's house to be with me. My mom arrived and the next day she, my aunt, and I went to the police station to talk with the detectives, subsequently, a warrant was issued for Maurice's arrest. Upon leaving the police station I called and canceled my bankcard, only to realize Maurice had depleted my entire account at the casino.

That night Maurice began calling me and apologizing. He stated he didn't know that he had injured me and was afraid to come back to the house because he knew the police would be there. We talked every night and he continued to apologize, vowing to stop drinking, doing drugs, and never putting his hands on me again. I told him that he would need to seek counseling and I would agree to give our relationship another chance. Maurice agreed and I moved back home even though the court case was pending.

Maurice made it appear that he had completely changed. He was more loving, caring, and attentive and he was no longer being verbally or physically abusive. Nevertheless, the changes were only because he was still going to court related to the domestic violence charges from me having to bleed around the brain. The closer it came to court Maurice continued to talk to me about the case and coerce me into saying the things he wanted me to say. This continued until the court hearing, while there I told the prosecutors everything Maurice wanted me to say, which resulted in him only receiving weekend time for a month.

Every Friday I would take him to the jail and pick him up on Sunday evening until the duration of his sentence was complete.

Losing Myself

~I began to feel depressed, worthless, and less attractive and contemplated killing myself just to be free from enduring any more hurt harm, or danger. ~

My life continued to change each day after I decided to take Maurice back. I realized that he would lie about any and everything, including never putting his hands on me. Once Maurice's weekend jail time and probation were complete, we moved to a new home hoping to have a clean slate and start our lives over. Every day brought new challenges and Maurice continued to divulge in alcohol and drugs. Maurice continued to come home irate becoming increasingly violent and more aggressive. I relished going to work because I felt more at peace, I was able to be around other people and get out of the house. As time progressed, I continued to work as well as attend a school where I met several acquaintances. In school I had a project that required me to partner with fellow students who were male and female, however, Maurice was displeased with this.

I came home from school letting Maurice know how

my day went when one of the group members called my phone. Maurice heard the voice on the phone was a male and he was extremely upset. He took my phone, broke it, then proceeded to hit me, pulling out my hair and placing a gun to my face. Maurice said that he would kill me while trying to make me open my mouth to put the gun inside of it. I moved and said no while screaming telling him to stop. Maurice finally stopped and he decided to leave the house. He came back the next morning apologizing indicating he wanted to talk after he left court, for a DUI. Maurice left for court and by the time he came back I had packed up the kids and things fleeing to a new apartment.

Maurice came to the house and realized we were gone, he was hysterical. He called my phone numerous times until I finally answered. I refused to let him know where we were staying and would only allow Maurice to meet at my job to pick up or drop off the kids. Each time he would see or call me he called me a bitch, hoe, fat, or ugly. Always criticizing me or saying something so demeaning to the point that it made me feel less than a woman. I began to feel depressed, worthless, and less attractive and contemplated killing myself just to be free from enduring any more hurt harm, or danger.

With every passing day, I began to feel like I was losing myself. I saw my family and friends less and less and my social life revolved around Maurice, his family, and friends. My days and nights began to run together, where all I would do is work, take care of my kids, and cater to Maurice. The physical abuse began to get worse each time from having black eyes, and being choked, to my body constantly being bruised all over. Not only did I suffer from being hit, but Maurice also forced me to have sexual intercourse when I didn't want to. It got so bad that one night I rejected having intercourse, so Maurice picked me up by the throat and threw me into the side of the bathtub. My head hit the side of the tub extremely hard causing the tub to break in half. He then pulled the gun, as he was yelling, he pulled the trigger and the gun fired. The bullet went flying throughout the bathroom bouncing off the walls and sink, causing a hole, until it landed in the wall next to the toilet.

A few days later, my dad came to my house to visit. While there, Maurice arrived at the house intoxicated cursing me out and trying to take the keys to my car. When I prevented Maurice from getting my keys, he threw a glass beer bottle at me. I signaled to my dad to call the police, so he stepped outside to make the call. Maurice walked outside behind him, taking his phone to prevent him from calling, so while they were outside, I contacted the police to come and de-escalate the situation. When the police arrived, they took our statement, instructed Maurice to leave for the night, and indicated if they came back, they would take both of us to jail. It was again at this moment that I began to lose faith in the justice system.

Physical Abuse of Child

~She ran into my bedroom screaming for me to help her as he jacked her up against the window constantly screaming, choking, and punching her. ~

Maurice always put fear in Tonya's, his oldest daughter, head making her either not want to date boys or sneak and do it without his knowledge. He would tell her if a boy were to come around, he would beat them up, grill them extremely hard, and they needed to have an appearance that was pleasing to him. However, there was a double standard when it came to his sons; Maurice would drink and smoke with them while encouraging them to talk with multiple girls. Knowing her father would disapprove, Tonya began talking to three boys she met at school, as well as online and her behavior began to slowly change. Maurice decided to wait to address his concerns with Tonya until after my scheduled surgery,

A couple of weeks after having surgery, we decided to go to Shelby Farms and have a picnic with the kids. We were all having a fun time until we started taking a hike thru the park's trail. Maurice decided this was the best time to go thru Tonya's phone to see what he could find to better understand the change in her behavior. While walking the trails, he instructed Tonya to walk in front of us with her younger sisters as he went thru the phone. As he began searching thru the phone, he came across inappropriate messages between Tonya and an older guy. One of the messages he found said "I like it when you do it rough, hit me, choke me but don't pull my hair." Maurice was livid when he saw this message, and he told her "You got me fucked up, I'm going to show you what that means." We came off the trail and began heading towards the car to leave the park as he continued to become increasingly mad. As we got into the truck to head home, Maurice got in the driver's seat and Tonya sat directly behind him. He was going off on her indicating he was going to whoop her when we got home. As soon as she tried to respond to him, he reached around the seat grabbing Tonya by the hair, pulling her hair so hard that he pulled it out.

When we made it home Tonya went to her room and undressed stating she knew he was going to get a belt and whoop her. Maurice proceeded to go into Tonya's room where he began to beat her. He punched and kicked her all over. She ran into my bedroom screaming for me to help her as he jacked her up against the window constantly screaming, choking, and punching her. Once he was done, she went into her room and cried herself to sleep. She awoke the next morning, preparing herself for school, sore all over and she had a bloodshot eye. I vowed to never let him harm my children or her ever again, I would do whatever it took to get away from him.

I never thought Maurice would stoop so low as to put his hands on our children. I've always said it's one thing to hurt me but to hurt our children is completely unacceptable. It became imperative that Tonya was sent to stay with her mother to ensure she was in a safe environment and Maurice couldn't harm her again.

Threats of Violence

~He wanted to run his truck thru the front door, kidnap me and shoot me in the face; he wanted to kill me in my sleep; he threatened to burn down our house and my family members' homes. ~

Maurice left the house at 9 am heading to his friend's house. He called throughout the day to check on the kids and me ensuring that we didn't need anything. I got up cooked, cleaned the house, picked the kids up from school, helped them with homework, and prepared them for bed. By 8 pm Maurice still hadn't made it home and had stopped answering his phone. I called him one last time, leaving a voice message saying I was going to bed. I was awakened, by my phone ringing at midnight, to Maurice saying he was on his way home. I went back to sleep and woke up to Maurice talking crazy, he climbed into bed and punched me in the face. I jumped up, grabbed my cellphone, and called 911. He took the phone out of my hand and threw it against the wall causing it to break. The 911 operator called back on the cell and since they didn't get a response, they began calling the house phone. Maurice would not let me out of the bedroom and was holding me hostage. I called for my kids to call the police. My oldest brought her phone to my bedroom door and when I tried to open the door Maurice snatched the phone from her hand and I was able to grab her and run into the kid's room. He followed me and grabbed me by the back of my neck trying to drag me back into the bedroom.

The police arrived and started knocking on the door and window. I ran to let up the garage and Maurice pushed me into the door letting the garage back down. I yelled outside telling the police they would have to break the door or window to get in since he wouldn't let us out of the house. I ran back into the kids' room and started knocking on their bedroom window to get the police's attention. They saw us and upon coming to the window my kids and I were able to escape to safety by climbing out of the window. The officers were able to make entry into the house by breaking the lock on the gate and breaking the handle off the back door. After entering the house, they found Maurice hiding in the hall closet, they arrested him and booked him into the county jail. The next morning Maurice bonded out of jail and a restraining order was put in place.

Over the next couple of days, Maurice would call repeatedly, he was irate because I called the police and had him arrested. He called, texted, and left voice messages throughout the entire day, constantly making threats on my life. There were messages indicating he wanted to run his truck thru the front door, kidnap me and shoot me in the face; he wanted to kill me in my sleep; he threatened to burn down our house and my family members' homes. I called the police to file a harassment report. The police arrived at my home to take a report, while taking my information Maurice began to call, and the officer instructed me to answer the call, placing it on the speaker to which I obliged. Once I answered the call Maurice began not only threatening me but making threats towards the police officer as well. When we went to court Maurice's bond was revoked and they held him until the trial date.

I was at a crossroads, do I take him back and forgive him because he is apologizing, or do I move forward, gaining my strength and voice back because he will apologize for a minute but go back and do it again. I knew that this was my time to finally get away from this abusive situation. I went to every court date even though Maurice would look at me saying he loved me and wanted me to work to have his charges dropped. Being able to get on the stand and tell what happened to me was a sigh of relief. Knowing I was able to stare my abuser in the face and say I am no longer afraid, and I can speak my truth, you no longer have a hold on me was the most invigorating feeling. I took back my power, my strength, my joy, my peace, and my life. Maurice was given a 10-year sentence plus probation after the end of the sentence plus he can have no further contact with me at all.

How I Got Away

Having a good support system or someone to support you no matter what, was what I needed. My family always said, "You have to leave him" or "Why did you go back to him?". It's not always as simple as it seems; especially when there are children involved. I began to realize that I was isolated from my family and friends and that he knew where my family lived. I went to a family member's house and Maurice threatened to burn the house down. It made me realize that if I went to see one of my family members, Maurice would do anything to find me, and I would put my family in jeopardy.

I thought about my children, and how they didn't grow up around anyone in my family, so they didn't have a bond with any of my family. I believed I didn't have help with them because I was working. Maurice made it to where he would take the girls to school, from school, and have them until I got off work. He made sure to make it to where I would need him or his family. I feared stepping out and doing things on my own because of the fear he instilled in me. I ensured my children were around my family more, which allowed them to become comfortable and grow an unbreakable bond with them.

I talked to friends and family about what I was going through in my marriage. It helps them understand all I've been through, as well as better understand why I rarely come around. They pass by my house every day to make sure everything is fine before I go home; stay with me to make sure that I am safe from injury, harm, or danger; and provide emotional support. My family was there with me every step of the way. They attended my hearings and made sure I didn't let Maurice's antics get in the way of me or convince me to drop the case.

Finally, I had to work on myself. After reaching a breaking point, I sought remedy with a psychologist to assist me get through the hurt and pain. Speaking with a therapist helped me identify ways to cope with things and ways to better express my thoughts and feelings. All these things helped me to escape from my abuser, now my ex-husband, and stay away.

Effects After Abuse

For 13 years my life and my children's lives changed forever. The abuse took a toll on me mentally, emotionally, and physically. I began to look at people differently, not knowing what to expect of them. I feared a male speaking loud or attempting to argue because I viewed it as a threat. It was hard for me to trust anyone, and I caught myself jumping to conclusions or always thinking the worst of a person. I thought I had to defend myself at all costs not realizing the things I'd endured were causing me to become someone else and I needed to learn how to channel my energy and not take things out on others. My emotions had gone thru so much hell and turmoil with being neglected, ridiculed, shut down, and even made to feel irrelevant. All the negativity from this toxic relationship made me lose my self-worth causing me to have a lot of doubt, insecurities, and negative sentiments about myself. After being put down so much and being told I was fat, ugly and no one would want me; I had to learn how to love myself again.

Not only did I have to endure those horrors, but my

children also had to go through this nightmare. It shakes them emotionally and psychologically. Seeing their mother suffer any kind of pain from their father scarred them for the rest of their lives. I have talked to my children to let them know that a man hitting a woman is not acceptable, while a woman hitting a man is also not acceptable. Witnessing abuse, my children became more vulnerable, afraid of their father and believing that's how men treat women.

Research shows that many children who experience domestic violence are also victims of physical abuse. Children who witness domestic violence or are victims of abuse often feel fear, terror, and helplessness. They grow up realizing that people who are strong and proactive are often very vulnerable and unable to protect themselves. Children who witness violence between their parents may also be at greater risk of violence in their later relationships. All forms of intimate partner violence are preventable – and the best way to prevent it is to teach and promote healthy, respectful, and non-violent relationships from an early age. It is important for children to understand and see what healthy relationships are like, to be able to identify the signs of unhealthy relationships and learn how to get out of the situation or relationship. badly, safely but confidently. Children need to understand the difference between a loving, healthy, and secure relationship and an unhealthy one, so they can make choices that support their health. Children need to learn early on that controlling behaviors are different from loving and protective. No one should threaten you in the name of love.

Now I show my kids how to recognize the signs of abuse, so they never go through what I did. Teaching them to love themselves and never look for happiness, authenticity, or contentment in a man. I want them to do better than me and know that I have weathered the storm. Although our healing may take a long time, we will come to a better place.

Post-Traumatic Stress Disorder (PTSD)

Avoid Thinking
of the Trauma

Avoid Talking
of the Trauma

Easily
Frightened

Negative
Mood

Negative
Thinking

Always
on Guard

Avoiding
Places

Avoiding
Activities

Flashbacks

Cannot
Concentrate

Aggressive
Behavior

Loss of Interest

Feeling Guilt
or Shame

Substance Abuse

Sleeping Difficulty

Bad Dreams

PTSD After Domestic Violence

A person experiencing a life-threatening event can develop PTSD, and this includes victims of domestic violence, who may experience varying degrees of fear, vulnerability, and helplessness. In many cases, the fear a victim feels after a traumatic event does not get dealt with immediately because the abuser lives nearby or is present in the victim's life regularly.

- Avoidance: Avoiding reminders or "triggers" of the traumatic event, such as people, places, thoughts, or events
- Arousal and reactivity: Sudden inexplicable anger, outbursts, difficulty being reached emotionally, feeling numb, trouble sleeping, and startling easily
- Reliving the event: Being confronted by the emotional trauma of the event suddenly and without an obvious reason, resulting in emotional outbursts, chills, heart palpitations, extreme anxiety, and other symptoms

According to the Diagnostic and Statistical Manual of Mental Disorders, there are four categories of symptoms of PTSD that include intrusive memories, avoidance of things and places that trigger negative responses, changes in mood, and changes in the state of arousal reactions. Just as each person's experience is unique, these symptoms will manifest differently for everyone. Here are some symptoms of PTSD resulting from domestic abuse:

- Flashbacks of episodes of abuse
- Uncontrollable thoughts about the abuse
- Recurring nightmares about domestic violence
- Difficulty falling asleep due to fear of the abuse
- Feeling distressed when something in the environment triggers thoughts about the abuse
- Making efforts to avoid thinking about the trauma
- Avoiding places and things that could trigger these thoughts, such as taking alternate routes while driving or not wanting to pursue certain activities
- Avoiding certain topics of conversation
- Trying to avoid disagreements or conflict
- changing your lifestyle to avoid potential causes for abuse

- Having difficulty maintaining relationships
- Feeling isolated, or choosing to isolate yourself
- Having trouble socializing with people you used to enjoy being around
- Having trouble participating in activities you used to enjoy
- Feeling hopeless, guilty, or ashamed
- Feeling depressed
- Being easily startled or agitated
- Feeling like you need to act defensively
- Having trouble trusting others

I continue to heal from domestic violence, I sought out therapy to help with the support of dealing with PTSD. I have learned how to process feelings of anger and fear. By understanding the abuse was not my fault. Finally, I am still learning how to deal with things that trigger a PTSD episode.

Impact of The Restraining Order

I suffered so much in my marriage but after leaving and obtaining a restraining order things intensified. I looked over my shoulder all the time, watched my surroundings, and changed my everyday patterns. There were times I felt the restraining was just a piece of paper because Maurice would show up to places where I was or show up to the house, the police were called but they couldn't do anything because he was already gone from the premises.

Maurice violated the restraining order several times. I called the police to inform them of the violation and they made notes to the file but indicated it was up to the District Attorney to say he violated the terms. I reached out to the probation office and was told there was nothing they could do. I believed I was not going to get any help and would possibly end up hurt or dead because of the threats Maurice was making. It took me calling the District Attorney over ten times, forwarding them the text messages that Maurice sent to me, and informing them of the police reports that were filed in order for them to research everything that was going on and to show that he violated the restraining order. I am thankful for having the restraining order in place, if I didn't, I wouldn't be here today.

The process of getting a Domestic Violence Restraining Order varies by state but is applied for through the local court system. It is different from other protection orders in that it is only granted after a court hearing where both parties are heard by the judge and present information and evidence. After the hearing, if a DVRO is granted, it typically lasts longer than other types of protection orders, sometimes remaining active for years

Cycle of Abuse

1 Tensions Building
Tensions increase, breakdown of communication, victim becomes fearful and feels the need to placate the abuser

4 Calm
Incident is "forgotten",
no abuse is taking place.
The "honeymoon" phase

2 Incident
Verbal, emotional & physical abuse.
Anger, blaming, arguing.
Threats. Intimidation.

3 Reconciliation
Abuser apologizes, gives excuses, blames the victim, denies the abuse occured, or says that it wasn't as bad as the victim claims

Stages of Abuse

Stage 1 Tension Building

Just before the abuse occurs, stress begins to develop between the couple. Abuser's behavior can be passive-aggressive and can lead to lack of communication. This victim changes behavior to prevent the abuser from becoming violent.

In this stage, Maurice would partake in alcohol, smoke marijuana, and snort cocaine. He continued to go out and began staying out late without communicating with me. The more he indulged in the behavior, the more I would recognize the changes. As time went on more aggression was shown and anything that would happen while he was out would cause tension between us once he made it home. I tried not to indulge in arguing with Maurice to keep confusion down.

Stage 2 Incident of Abuse

The abuser will commit acts of domestic abuse like hitting, kicking, shoving, or throwing objects at their partner. Other kinds of abuse can also be portrayed such as sexual, emotional, stalking, intimidating, or practicing any other kind of extreme controlling behavior.

Whatever incident that would happen while Maurice was out, he would come home and take it out on me. I would try to go to sleep before he came home to prevent anything from happening, although that didn't help. Maurice would call and talk sweet to me but when he made it home his whole demeanor would change. He would come in punch me, choke me, and some nights force, me to have sex. I'd never imagined that I would not only be physically abused but also sexually abused by my spouse.

Stage 3 Reconciliation

The abuser becomes contrite and apologizes for their behavior. They become attentive or affectionate, they may try to ignore what happened or try to blame the victim for the acts of violence. They make promises or swear the abusive behavior will never happen again.

The next morning Maurice would apologize for his actions. There were some instances where he'd say he didn't remember everything that happened, or it was my fault for not doing what he wanted me to do. He never took accountability for his actions.

Stage 4 Calm

The abuser shows kindness to the victim while resisting the urge to fall back into the abusive behavior. Everything seems calm and peaceful, leading the victim to believe the abuser has changed. This is what I called the calm before the storm.

Things would go back to the way it was when we first met. He was so loving, caring, and attentive. We would have family outings with our kids, and I honestly thought things had changed.

Red Flags of a Domestic Violence Abuser

➢ Comes on as a real charmer and loves you instantly

➢ Doesn't like authority figures

➢ Embarrasses you in the presence of others

➢ Feels others competing with him or her and they must always win

➢ Wants your undivided attention all the time

➢ Controlling and must always be "in charge"

➢ Has a dual personality (adult or childish; Dr. Jekyll or Mr. Hyde)

➢ Promises and apologies are meaningless

➢ Displays jealously towards close friends and family

➢ Can't tolerate criticism and tries to justify unacceptable behavior

➢ Rough at times – love pats become more painful. Suddenly, you realize he or she is a serious abuser, and you are a victim

Break The Chains of Abuse

A man may speak to his wife in the same derogatory and disdainful tone that his father spoke to his mother, and a woman may passively succumb to her husband's demands, just like her mother. If your spouse is abused as a child, you will experience the same type of abuse. No matter how well-meaning the person is, it can explode with the same anger as a child. Anger can surface when you drink too much, be provoked, or become abused. Abuser's never change their behavior, but you can change the way you respond.

The most difficult part of an abusive relationship is breaking the cycle of abusiveness. The constant apologies and regrets of your partner can make it exceedingly difficult to break up and follow your separate path. He apologized many times. He bought you roses, made you a truly romantic supper, and even wrote beautiful love poems. "He's not a violent man," you think. "There is no way he can hurt me again." But surely, he experiences the same move again and closes the cycle of violence. The longer you stay in this dangerous abusive relationship, the more violent he becomes and the harder it is for you to get things done. You may soon become more depressed and anxious and begin to believe his lies as he thinks his violent behavior is justified and worthy of it.

There is no excuse for domestic violence. none. But in many cases, women are the victims. They don't want to believe that their partner is abusive, so they look past the first blow and keep the cycle of abuse in earnest. Being attentive, strong, and communicative will break the cycle of violence and enable women to continue their lives.

Abusive Behavior

➤ Telling you that you never do anything right. Blames others a lot, and often it's you.

➤ Showing extreme jealousy of your friends or time spent away from them.

➤ Preventing, discouraging, or isolating you from spending time with friends, family members, or peers. Every time you mention something that you would like to do outside of them, without them involved then it's, 'I was going to take you to dinner; I just want us to spend a quiet night at home.'

➤ Insulting, demeaning, belittling, or shaming you, especially in front of other people; even when joking.

➤ Preventing you from making your own decisions, including about working or attending school.

➤ Controlling finances in the household without discussion, including taking your money or refusing to provide money for necessary expenses.

➤ Pressuring you to have sex or perform sexual acts you're not comfortable with.

- Pressuring you to use drugs or alcohol.
- Alcohol and drug use that causes erratic behavior can be a catalyst for abuse
- Intimidating you through threatening looks or actions. Instills fear, uneasiness, or are intimidating in their speech or actions.
- Insulting your parenting or threatening to harm or take away your children or pets.
- Intimidating you with weapons like guns, knives, bats, or mace.
- Destroying your belongings or your home.
- They manipulate your emotions and make you feel guilty.
- They get physical. Hitting someone is abusive, but physical abuse can start as intimidating posturing, grabbing, or controlling your movements and space.

TYPES OF DOMESTIC ABUSE

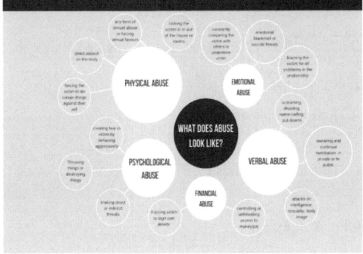

Learn the Warning Signs

Domestic violence victims try to cover up the abuse for a variety of reasons and learning the warning signs of domestic abuse can help you help them.

Physical Signs:

- Black eyes
- Busted lips
- Red or purple marks on the neck
- Sprained wrists
- Bruises on the arms

Emotional Signs:

- Low self-esteem
- Overly apologetic or meek
- Fearful
- Changes in sleeping or eating patterns
- Anxious or on edge
- Substance abuse
- Symptoms of depression

- Loss of interest in once enjoyed activities and hobbies
- Talking about suicide

Behavioral Signs:
- Becoming withdrawn or distant
- Canceling appointments or meetings at the last minute
- Being late often
- Excessive privacy concerning their personal life
- Isolating themselves from friends and family

How to Help Someone Going Thru Domestic Violence

The effects of being in an abusive relationship are devastating for the victim. Looking in from the outside can be difficult, and there are always questions you may have. You may ask the following: Why do they stay? Why does he or she keep going back? What can I do to help?

As a loved one or friend there are things to consider when helping or supporting the domestic violence victim:

- ➤ Listen to and believe your loved one. Allow them to control their own lives. If your loved one does not want to leave or call the police, do not force them to.
- ➤ Do not get involved in their fights, as doing so may endanger you. Call the police instead.
- ➤ Offer your loved one a safe place to stay or help him or her get to a shelter.
- ➤ Be there to support them. Don't criticize them or cause them to shut down.

- Seek privacy so your loved one is protected from disclosing in public.
- Don't judge them for going back. Explore the reasons they decided to stay or go back and offer help. If childcare or finances are a concern, for instance, try offering financial assistance.

What Not to Do

Although there is no right or wrong way to help a victim of domestic violence, you want to avoid doing anything that will make the situation worse.

Don't...

- Bash the abuser. Focus on the behavior, not the personality.
- Judge or blame the victim. That's what the abuser does.
- Underestimate the potential danger for the victim and yourself.
- Promise any help that you can't follow through with.
- Give conditional support.
- Do anything that might provoke the abuser.
- Pressure the victim.
- Give up. If they are not willing to open up at first, be patient.
- Do anything to make it more difficult for the victim.
- Judge the victim.
- Talk or gossip about the victim with others.

"WHY DOES SHE STAY?"

WHY THIS IS THE WRONG QUESTION TO ASK

Understand the Reasons Why Victims Stay

It can be hard to understand why someone you care about would choose to stay in an abusive or unhealthy relationship. Here are a few reasons why it's not easy to part ways.

- Fear of harm if they leave
- They still love their partner and believe they will change
- Their partner promised to change
- A strong belief that marriage is "for better or worse"
- Thinking the abuse is their fault
- Staying for the children
- Lack of self-confidence
- Fear of isolation or loneliness
- Pressure from family, community, or church
- Lack of means (job, money, transportation) to survive on their own
- Help the victim find support and resources.
- Look up numbers for shelters, social services, attorneys, counselors, or support groups. If available,

offer brochures or pamphlets about domestic violence.

- You'll also want to help them get information on any laws regarding protective orders/restraining orders and child custody information. You can search state by state for legal information on WomensLaw.org.
- If the victim asks you to do something specific and you are willing to do it, don't hesitate to help.

Some thoughts and questions about why the victim stay:

1. **If it is so bad, why doesn't he/she leave?** Leaving or ending a relationship is not an easy decision. The relationship may hold a lot of emotional value to the individual. If there are children, the individual could experience economic hardship due to financial dependency. He/she may not realize the resources available in the area. There is a possibility that the abuser used violence to prevent the victim from leaving.

2. **Lately he/she has been distant:** An abuser believes that a partner with fewer relationships can be more

easily controlled. The abuser may be extremely jealous of any relationships the partner has outside the home. The victim distances themselves from friends or family fearing they will discover the violence and they would be blamed for it.

3. **The violence can't be that serious:** Domestic violence can contain threats, pushing, punching, choking, sexual attack, and attack with weapons. Over time those attacks can expand in severity. A lot of those attacks require scientific interest, but scientific interest is in no way sought.

4. **Are children involved?** It can be difficult to leave when children are involved. After being separated from anyone, it becomes difficult to escape with children. He/she looks at the school situation, whereas the other parent or partner gets the children to and from school. The victim feels helpless, especially after leaving the circle of their relatives and friends. The abuser may also have used intimidation to prevent the victim from taking the child, and the victim does not have to leave the child.

5. **Why doesn't he or she stay with family?** Having a safe place to stay is very important to the victim. There may be times when the victim tries to stay with their family but is turned away by them. The victim may be afraid to go to the family because the abuser may find her there. The abuser could have threatened the victim's family's life if he had gone there.

6. **What are the most dangerous times for a woman in an abusive relationship?** When she's pregnant (the abuser may see the baby as an intruder and a competitor for her attention). When the victim tells the abuser that she is leaving. Victims should give no signs that they intend to leave. During the first 2 years after departure.

Domestic Violence Safety Plan

A COMPREHENSIVE PLAN THAT WILL KEEP YOU SAFER WHETHER YOU STAY OR LEAVE

Form a Safety Plan

Contacting a trained domestic violence advocate near you is the best way to create a safety plan. An advocate can help you navigate the steps and find local resources, including shelters, support groups, and legal and financial assistance. You can also assist the victim in creating a safety plan that can be implemented if violence occurs again or if they decide to leave. Taking the time to plan can help them visualize the steps they need to take and to mentally prepare for them. Victims who leave their abusive partners are at a greater risk of dying in their abuser's arms than those who stay. Therefore, it is extremely important for a victim to develop a personalized safety plan before a crisis happens or before deciding to leave. Work with the victim to develop a safety plan, weighing the risks and benefits of each option and identifying ways to reduce the risks.

Be sure to include the following in the safety plan:

- A safe place to go in an emergency, or if they decide to leave home
- A prepared excuse to leave if they feel threatened

- A code word to alert family or friends that you need help
- An "escape bag" with cash, important documents (birth certificates, social security cards), keys, toiletries, and a change of clothes that can be easily accessed
- A list of emergency contacts, including trusted family or friends, local shelters, and domestic abuse hotline

Planning an escape route

 Packing an emergency bag

 Storing money

 Making copies of important documents (e.g. passport, bank statement, proof of residency)

 Making arrangements for animals

"Breaking the Cycle of Abuse." *Psychology Today*, Sussex Publishers, https://www.psychologytoday.com/us/blog/the-compassion-chronicles/202006/breaking-the-cycle-abuse.

"Domestic Violence Statistics: A Comprehensive Investigation." *Dolan + Zimmerman LLP*, 5 Apr. 2022, https://www.dolanzimmerman.com/domestic-violence-statistics/.

Gluck, S. (2021, December 17). Cycle of Violence and Abuse and How to Break the Cycle of Abuse, HealthyPlace. Retrieved on 2022, June 13 from https://www.healthyplace.com/abuse/domestic-violence/cycle-of-violence

"Home: Office on Women's Health." *Home | Office on Women's Health*, https://www.womenshealth.gov/.

"Mental Health Treatment & Drug Rehab." *High Focus Centers*, 31 Mar. 2022, https://highfocuscenters.pyramidhealthcarepa.com/.

"NCADV: National Coalition Against Domestic Violence." *The Nation's Leading Grassroots Voice on Domestic Violence*, https://ncadv.org/STATISTICS.

"Plain-Language Legal Information for Victims of Abuse." *WomensLaw.org*, 1 June 2022, https://www.womenslaw.org/.

Roxanne Dryden-Edwards, MD. "Domestic Violence Types, Effects, Warning Signs & Hotline." *MedicineNet*, 2 May 2022, https://www.medicinenet.com/domestic_violence/article.htm.

"The Connection between Domestic Violence and PTSD." *Beaufort Memorial Hospital*, https://www.bmhsc.org/blog/the-connection-between-domestic-violence-and-ptsd.

"Warning Signs of Abuse." *The Hotline*, 3 Feb. 2022, https://www.thehotline.org/identify-abuse/domestic-abuse-warning-signs/-and-abuse-and-how-to-break-the-cycle-of-abuse

Made in the USA
Columbia, SC
20 September 2022

67070767R00046